THE STENCIL COLLECTION
Wild Flow
Katrina Hall

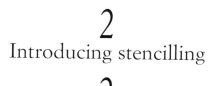

C000097949

Dandelions   8

Poppies   12

Forget-me-nots   16

Daisy & Wild Rose Buds   20

Cornflowers & Butterflies   24

Fritillary   28

INTRODUCING STENCILLING

Once you begin stencilling you will be amazed at the wonderful results you can obtain quite easily and without spending a great deal of money. This book introduces six themed projects and provides ready-to-use stencils that can be used with numerous variations in design – just follow the step-by-step features and simple instructions. With very little paint and only a few pieces of equipment you can achieve stunning results. Have fun!

BASIC MATERIALS

Paints and Decorative Finishes
Emulsion paint*
Water-based stencil paint
Oil sticks
Acrylic paints (bottles and tubes)
Specialist paints (for fabrics, ceramics, glass etc)
Spray paints
Metallic acrylic artists' colours (gold, silver etc)
Silver and gold art flow pens
Bronze powders (various metallics)
Gilt wax

Brushes and Applicators
Art brushes (variety of sizes)
Stencil brushes (small, medium and large)
Sponge applicators
Mini-roller and tray
*Australian readers should use matt acrylic paint instead

Other Equipment
Set square
Blotting paper
Scissors or scalpel (or craft knife)
Roll of lining paper (for practising)
Eraser
Soft pencil
Fine-tip permanent pen
Chalk or Chalkline and powdered chalk
Long rigid ruler
Tape measure
Plumbline
Spirit level
Low-tack masking tape
Spray adhesive
Tracing paper
Paint dishes or palettes
Cloths
Kitchen roll
White spirit or mineral turpentine
Stencil plastic or card
Cotton buds
Methylated spirits

CUTTING OUT STENCILS
The stencils at the back of the book are all designed to be used separately or together to create different pattern combinations. Cut along the dotted lines of the individual stencils and make sure you transfer the reference code onto each one with a permanent pen. Carefully remove the cut-out pieces of the stencil. Apply 50 mm (2 in) strips of tracing paper around the edges using masking tape; this will help to prevent smudging paint onto your surface.

REPAIRING STENCILS
Stencils may become damaged and torn from mishandling, or if the cutouts have not been removed carefully, but they are easy to repair. Keeping the stencil perfectly flat, cover both sides of the tear with masking tape. Then carefully remove any excess tape with a scalpel.

GETTING STARTED

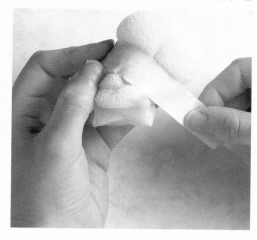

DUPLICATING STENCILS

Stencil plastic (Mylar) can be used; or card wiped over with linseed oil, which left to dry will harden and make the surface waterproof. Place the cut-out stencil on top. Trace around carefully with a permanent pen inside the cut-out shapes. Cut along the lines with a scalpel and remove the pieces. You may prefer to trace on top of the design, then transfer your tracing onto card.

MAKING A SPONGE APPLICATOR

Sponging your stencil is one of the easiest methods, but you may prefer to use a stencil brush, especially for fine detail. Using a piece of upholstery foam or very dense bath sponge, cut pieces 12–50 mm ($^1/_2$–2 in) wide and approximately 50 mm (2 in) long. Hold the four corners together and secure with tape to form a pad. You can also round off the ends with scissors or a scalpel and trim to a smooth finish. The small-ended applicators can be used for tiny, intricate patterns.

HOW TO USE WATER-BASED PAINT

Water-based paints are easy and economical to use and have the advantage of drying quickly. For professional-looking stencils, do not load your sponge or brush too heavily or you will not achieve a soft, shaded finish. Paint that is too watery will seep under the stencil edges and smudge. If the paint is too heavy you will obtain a heavy block effect rather than the soft stippling you require.

LOOKING AFTER STENCILS

Stencils have a long life if cared for correctly. Before cleaning make sure you remove any tape or tracing paper that has been added. Remove any excess paint before it dries, and wipe the stencil with a damp cloth every time you use it. If water or acrylic paint has dried and hardened, soften it with water and ease it off gently with a scalpel. Then use a small amount of methylated spirits on a cloth to remove the rest. An oil-based paint can simply be removed by wiping over the stencil with white spirit on a cloth. Stencils should be dried thoroughly before storing flat between sheets of greaseproof paper.

HOW TO USE OIL STICKS

Oil sticks may seem expensive, but in fact go a long way. They take longer to dry, allowing you to blend colours very effectively. Oil sticks are applied with a stencil brush and you need to have a different brush for each colour. Break the seal as instructed on the stick and rub a patch of the colour onto a palette, allowing space to blend colours. As the stencil sticks dry slowly, you need to lift the stencil off cleanly, and replace to continue the pattern.

PRACTISING PAINTING STENCILS

Roll out some lining paper onto a table and select the stencil you wish to practise with. Using spray adhesive, lightly spray the back of your stencil and place it into position on the paper. Prepare your paint on a palette. Dab your sponge or brush into the paint and offload excess paint onto scrap paper. Apply colour over the stencil in a light coat to create an even stippled effect. You can always stencil on a little more paint if a stronger effect is needed, but if you over apply it in the first place it is very difficult to remove. Keep separate sponges for different colours.

PLANNING YOUR DESIGN

Before starting to stencil take time to plan your design. Decide where you want to use the patterns, then work out how to position the stencils so that the design will fit around obstacles such as doorways and corners. The techniques shown here will help you to undertake the job with a systematic approach.

PUTTING PATTERN PIECES TOGETHER

1 Before you apply your design, stencil a sample onto lining paper. Mark the centre and baseline of the design on the paper and put together your pattern pieces. You can then work out the size of the design, how it will fit into the space available and the distance required between repeats.

2 You can avoid stencilling around a corner by working out the number of pattern repeats needed, and allowing extra space either between repeats or within the pattern. Creating vertical lines through the pattern will allow you to stretch it evenly.

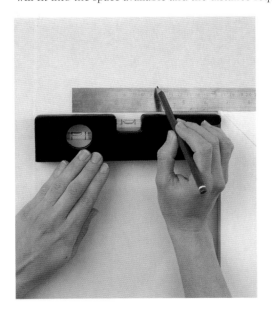
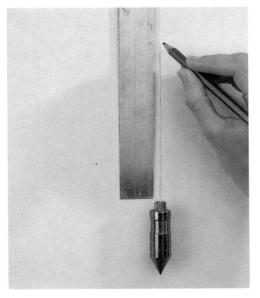

MARKING BASELINES AND HORIZONTAL LINES

Select your stencil area, and take a measure from the ceiling, doorframe, window or edging, bearing in mind the depth of your stencil. Using a spirit level, mark out a horizontal line. You can then extend this by using a chalkline or long ruler with chalk or soft pencil.

MARKING VERTICAL LINES

If you need to work out the vertical position for a stencil, hang a plumbline above the stencilling area and use a ruler to draw a vertical line with chalk or a soft pencil. You will need to use this method when creating an all-over wallpaper design.

FIXING THE STENCIL INTO PLACE

Lightly spray the back of the stencil with spray adhesive, then put it in position and smooth it down carefully. You can use low-tack masking tape if you prefer, but take care not to damage the surface to be stencilled; keep the whole stencil flat to prevent paint seeping underneath.

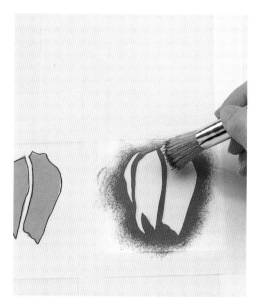

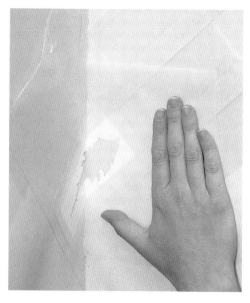

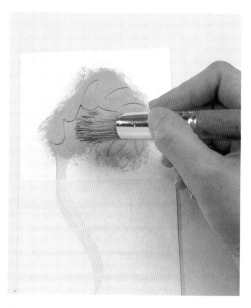

MARKING THE STENCIL FOR A PATTERN REPEAT

Attach a border of tracing paper to each edge of the stencil. Position the next pattern and overlap the tracing paper onto the previous design, tracing over the edge of it. By matching the tracing with the previous pattern as you work along you will be able to align and repeat the stencil at the same intervals.

COPING WITH CORNERS

Stencil around corners after you have finished the rest of the design, having measured to leave the correct space for the corner pattern before you do so. Then bend the stencil into the corner and mask off one side of it. Stencil the open side and allow the paint to dry, then mask off this half and stencil the other part to complete the design.

MASKING OFF PART OF A STENCIL

Use low-tack masking tape to mask out small or intricate areas of stencil. You can also use ordinary masking tape, but remove excess stickiness first by peeling it on and off your skin or a cloth once or twice. To block off inside shapes and large areas, cut out pieces of tracing paper to the appropriate size and fix them on top with spray adhesive.

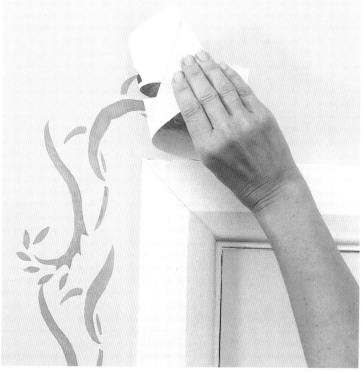

MITRING STENCIL PATTERNS

1 When you are stencilling a continuous pattern and need to make a corner, mask off the stencil by marking a 45-degree angle at both ends of the stencil with a permanent pen. Mask along this line with a piece of masking tape or tracing paper.

2 Make sure the baselines of the stencil on both sides of the corner are the same distance from the edge, and that they cross at the corner. Put the diagonal end of the stencil right into the corner and apply the paint. Turn the stencil sideways to align the other diagonal end of the stencil and turn the corner.

PAINT EFFECTS

CHOOSING COLOURS

Take care to choose appropriate colours to create the effect you want. Stencil a practice piece onto paper and try a variation of colours to ensure you are pleased with the result. Different colours can make a design look entirely different. Use spray adhesive to fix your practice paper onto the surface on which you wish to produce the design so that you can assess its effect before applying the stencil.

APPLYING WATER-BASED COLOURS

Water-based paint dries quickly, so it tends to layer rather than blend. It is best applied by using a swirling movement or gently dabbing, depending on the finished effect you wish to create. Once you have applied a light base colour, you can add a darker edge for shading. Alternatively, leave some of the stencil bare and add a different tone to that area to obtain a shaded or highlighted appearance.

BLENDING OIL-STICK COLOURS

Oil sticks mix together smoothly and are perfect for blending colours. Place the colours separately on your palette and mix them with white to obtain a variety of tones or blend them together to create new colours. You can also blend by applying one coat into another with a stippling motion while stencilling. Blending looks most effective when applying a pale base coat, then shading on top with a darker colour.

HIGHLIGHTING

A simple way to add highlighting to your design is first to paint in your stencil in a light tone of your main colour, then carefully lift the stencil and move it down a fraction. Then stencil in a darker shade; this leaves the highlighted areas around the top edges of the pattern.

GILDING

After painting your stencil use gold to highlight the edges. Load a fine art brush with gold acrylic paint and carefully outline the top edges of the pattern. Use one quick brush stroke for each pattern repeat, keeping in the same direction. Other methods are to blow bronze powder onto the wet paint, draw around the pattern with a gold flow pen, or smudge on gilt wax cream, then buff to a high sheen.

APPLYING SPRAY PAINTS

Spray paints are ideal on glass, wood, metal, plastic and ceramic surfaces. They are quick to apply and fast drying, but cannot be blended, although you can achieve subtle shaded effects. Apply the paint in several thin coats. Mask off a large area around the design to protect it from the spray, which tends to drift. Try to use sprays out of doors or in a well-ventilated area. Some spray paints are non-toxic, making them ideal for children's furniture.

DIFFERENT SURFACES

BARE WOOD

Rub the wood surface down to a smooth finish. Then fix the stencil in place and paint with a thin base coat of white, so that the stencil colours will stand out well when applied. Leave the stencil in place and allow to dry thoroughly, then apply your stencil colours in the normal way. When completely dry you can apply a coat of light wax or varnish to protect your stencil.

PAINTED WOOD

If you are painting wood or medium-density fibreboard (MDF) prior to stencilling, seal it with a coat of acrylic primer before adding a base coat of emulsion or acrylic paint. If the base coat is dark, stencil a thin coat of white paint on top. Apply your stencil and, if required, protect with a coat of clear varnish when it is completely dry.

FABRIC

Use special fabric paint for stencilling on fabric and follow the manufacturer's instructions carefully. Place card or blotting paper behind the fabric while working and keep the material taut. If you are painting a dark fabric, best results are achieved by stencilling first with white or a lighter shade. Heat seal the design following the manufacturer's instructions.

CERAMICS

Use special ceramic paints to work directly onto glazed ceramic tiles, and unglazed ceramics such as terracotta. Make sure all surfaces are clean, so that the stencils can be fixed easily. Apply the paint with a brush, sponge, spray or mini-roller. Ceramic paints are durable and washable, and full manufacturer's instructions are given on the container.

GLASS

Before applying the stencil make sure the glass is clean, spray on a light coat of adhesive and place the stencil in position. Spray on water-based or ceramic paint, remove the stencil and allow to dry. If you wish to stencil drinking glasses, use special non-toxic and water-resistant glass paints. An etched-glass look with stencils on windows, doors and mirrors can be achieved with a variety of materials.

PAINTED SURFACES

Stencils can be applied to surfaces painted with matt, satin or vinyl silk emulsion, oil scumble glazes, acrylic glazes and varnishes, and to matt wallpaper. If you wish to decorate a gloss surface, stencil first with an acrylic primer, leave to dry and then stencil the colours on top. Surfaces to be stencilled need to be smooth so that the stencil can lay flat.

DANDELIONS

Most gardeners have a love/hate relationship with the dandelion – this flower grows and spreads like wild fire, plaguing lawns with long roots that are extremely difficult to dig up. To children, however, dandelions are heaven-sent to 'tell the time' by blowing the feathery seed heads on summer afternoons. A mesh cupboard is an ideal piece for this project, giving it a 'potting shed' feel. The leaves and flowers are joined to create dandelion plants growing from the bottom of the cupboard, with seeds floating above and a snail sneaking in.

PAINT COLOUR GUIDE

White spray paint

DECORATING THE CUPBOARD DOORS

1 Paint the cupboard wood sections with an all-in-one primer/undercoat in white. Paint a couple of layers of white emulsion on top. You may be able to get away with just one layer depending how thick the paint is.

2 Make up a wash by diluting a stone-coloured emulsion with water. Put the colour on and carefully drag it off with a dry brush to give an 'old' wood effect. Work the paint in the direction of the wood sections of the cupboard, emphasizing the joints. When dry, give the wood a few coats of varnish.

3 The door knobs are stones with holes through the middle, tied on with string.

4 Paint the dandelion stencils on the mesh using white spray paint. Practise on a spare piece of mesh. If you make a mistake try mixing up a bit of silver and black paint to neaten the edges.

PROJECT PATTERN

The dandelion plants are built up by combining the different leaves and stalks (used in reverse and upside-down), topped with flowers and seed heads (dandelion clocks). The seeds are in the same pattern on each side although the overall look is random.

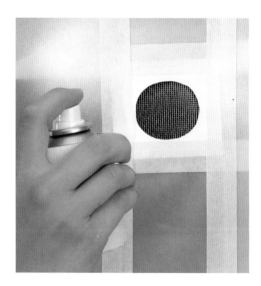

SPRAYING THE BASE COLOUR
Make sure that the stencils are fixed securely with spray adhesive, then spray the paint in thin layers to give a well-defined edge. Spray the background of the seed head stencil D lightly to give the faint impression of a globe before painting the individual seeds stencil A on top.

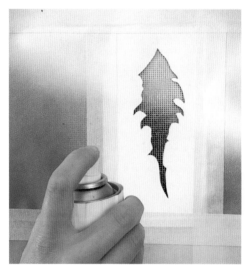

BUILDING UP LAYERS
To achieve a more opaque finish, spray lightly building up thin layers. Make sure that each element is dry before you move on to the next. Be careful not to over spray as the mesh holes can clog up easily.

CREATING THE SNAIL STENCIL
Use the snail stencil E to create a trail round a pot, along the front of shelves or on top of skirting boards. A simple element in a single colour can be low key or dramatic depending on the colour you use and how densely you apply it.

DANDELIONS VARIATIONS

This project provides endless opportunities for creative decoration. You can use greens and yellows to form realistic-looking dandelion plants or, as shown here using greens, turquoises and blues, choose the individual elements to build up many other designs. Do not be afraid to experiment with the different shapes as pure pattern rather than restricting yourself to the realistic growth pattern of the actual plant.

STAR EDGING (STENCIL A)

LEAF CIRCLE (STENCIL J)

SNAIL TRAIL (STENCIL E)

LEAF BORDER (STENCIL J)

SEED HEAD DESIGN (STENCILS A, D, F AND H)

LEAF WHEEL (STENCIL G)

SNOWFLAKE MOTIF (STENCIL B)

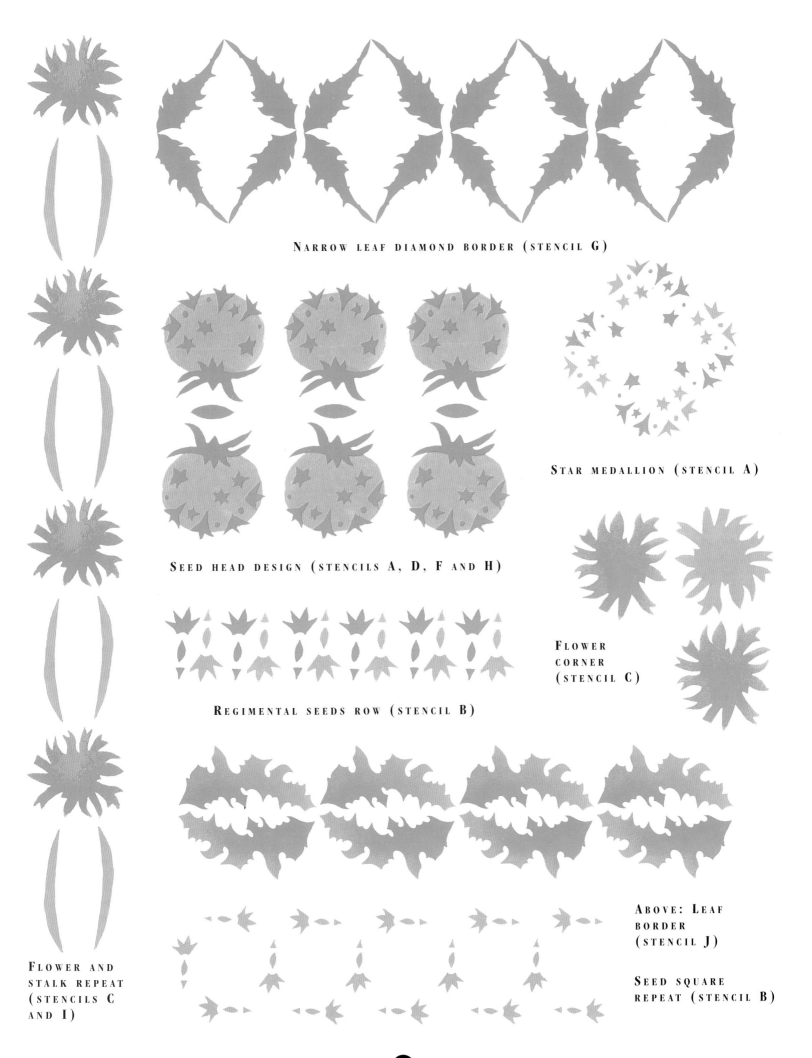

NARROW LEAF DIAMOND BORDER (STENCIL **G**)

STAR MEDALLION (STENCIL **A**)

SEED HEAD DESIGN (STENCILS **A**, **D**, **F** AND **H**)

FLOWER CORNER (STENCIL **C**)

REGIMENTAL SEEDS ROW (STENCIL **B**)

ABOVE: LEAF BORDER (STENCIL **J**)

SEED SQUARE REPEAT (STENCIL **B**)

FLOWER AND STALK REPEAT (STENCILS **C** AND **I**)

POPPIES

Poppies, to me, conjure up the quintessential hazy feeling of a high summer's day. In this project the combination of yellow ochre, deep purple, red and fiery orange creates a harmonious warm atmosphere. Spiky leaves, curvaceous poppy flowers with dark seductive centres, rounded seed heads, gently bending buds and bumble bees fuse to form a sympathetic union of shapes. Together the colours and shapes convey the feeling of walking through a golden field of corn, dotted with the richness of red and orange wild flowers.

PAINT COLOUR GUIDE

Deep purple   Dark red   Fiery orange

PAINTING THE FRAME

1 Paint the frame with all-in-one primer/undercoat and then paint two layers of yellow ochre emulsion.

2 Mix up a wash, with the consistency of single cream, using a burnt umber acrylic and emulsion glaze. Gently apply the wash with big brush strokes, working across the frame so that there is a hint of colour.

3 Apply the large poppy (stencils E, G and F) in the corners of the frame and add the other elements in a random pattern. Finish the frame by painting the inner and outer edges with a rich red to give the sides definition.

PROJECT PATTERN

In this random design the most difficult element is the poppy flower. Place stencil E first and then put stencil G carefully on top. Finish with stencil F, to complete the flower.

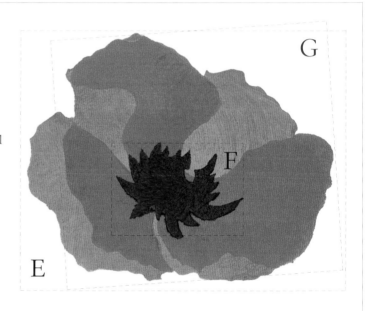

POSITIONING WITH CUTOUTS

To position the stencils make cutouts in paper and move the shapes around till you are happy with the design. Start with the larger shapes to get the pattern going and fill in the gaps with the smaller ones. Let some shapes overlap the frame.

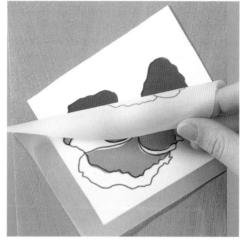

CHECKING WITH TRACING PAPER

To create the large poppy petals apply stencil G over stencil E. Position the two parts by using tracing paper to make a drawing of the way that the shapes fit together. Slide the top shape stencil G under the tracing paper, then remove the paper.

KEEPING COLOURS CLEAN

When using two colours within the same shape work from opposite ends of the stencil with them. Combine the colours in the middle with a different brush to keep the tones clean and clear.

POPPIES VARIATIONS

By adding pinks and yellow ochre to your palette of rich reds, oranges and purples you can move the design of this project towards the Orient to give a more mysterious feel or to India for a more exotic look. If you are adventurous you could make realistic poppy plants look as if they are growing out of the skirting boards or create entire poppy fields on the walls.

SEED HEAD EDGING (STENCIL C)

LEAF ZIGZAG (STENCIL A)

LEFT: POPPY CENTRE DESIGN (STENCIL F)   ABOVE: BEE REPEAT (STENCIL B)

POPPY BUD AND LEAF TILE BORDER (STENCILS A AND D)

POPPY HEAD REPEAT (STENCILS E, F AND G)

BUZZING BEES (STENCIL B)

LEAF TILE (STENCIL A)

**POPPY BUD TILE
(STENCIL D)**

LINKED POPPY BUD BORDER (STENCIL D)

**SEED HEAD
STRIPE
(STENCIL C)**

**POPPY BUD
BORDER
(STENCIL D)**

PAINT COLOUR GUIDE

Cobalt blue   Deep purple

Lime green   White

DECORATING WOODEN BOXES

1 Coat the raw wood with all-in-one primer/undercoat, then top it with a thin layer of baby blue. This may need a couple of coats with a sanding session in between to give a smooth surface.

2 Practise the design on paper to make sure all the elements fit. If you make a mistake on the box it is quite an art to patch it up. When you are ready stencil your design.

3 Stencilled surfaces benefit from at least two layers of varnish for protection. Water-based varnish is usually sufficient, but use oil-based varnish for a surface that will receive heavy use or needs to be heat resistant.

FORGET-ME-NOTS

Forget-me-nots twist and twine their way in amongst all the other wild flowers of the hedgerows and woodlands. These delicate-looking flowers seem to grow wild where gardens end and bluebell woods begin – that magical place where fairies dance. Combine blues, purples and greens with white flower centres to keep the project looking clean and fresh. A continuous row around the tops of the boxes links the design although the boxes are decorated differently.

PROJECT PATTERN

The border on both boxes is a simple repeat of stencil C. For the small box pattern rotate stencil D. The design on the large box is achieved by combining small sections with whole stencils.

DOUBLE-LAYERING THE PAINT
To achieve the effect of double-layered paint, put on the first coat and allow it to dry thoroughly. Reposition the stencil, then put on the second colour with a very dry brush using big swirling movements.

CHECKING THE COLOURS
Turn back the edge of a stencil to have a sneak preview of the colours and check the effect. You may want to add colour or depth here and there and it is easier to alter while the stencil is still in position.

PLACING THE FLOWER CENTRES
Use a cotton bud to add the flower centres. The best way is to paint a piece of paper in white and then use it as a paint reservoir to regulate your paint quantity. It is surprising how little paint you need.

FORGET-ME-NOTS VARIATIONS

The natural colours of these flowers range from light blue through mauves and pinks, giving you much room to experiment. Try adding turquoise and yellow to blues and lime greens. Do not feel restricted by the small nature of the forget-me-nots pattern. It could easily be transformed into a wide border or onto the panels of a door or around a hat box.

STALK AND LEAF OVALS (STENCIL E)

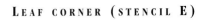

LEAF CORNER (STENCIL E)

CURLING STALKS (STENCIL E)

ENTWINED STALKS (STENCIL A)

FORGET-ME-NOT MOTIF (STENCIL D)

CURLING SPRIGS (STENCIL B)

LINKING TENDRILS MOTIF (STENCIL **A**)

FORGET-ME-NOT BORDER (STENCIL **B**)

CURLING SPRIGS STRIPE (STENCIL **B**)

TENDRILS RIBBON (STENCIL **A**)

FORGET-ME-NOT SWAGS (STENCIL **D**)

CHAIN OF FLOWERS (STENCIL **C**)

PAINT COLOUR GUIDE

Lime green   Brilliant white

Pinkish red   Bright yellow

PAINTING THE HEADBOARD

1 Sand the whole headboard well before you start – nothing could be worse than leaning on sharp wooden edges.

2 Give the headboard a couple of layers of emulsion paint to cover up any existing paintwork. Once the paintwork has dried apply a light green glaze.

3 It is worth testing the glaze with the stencil colours on top. In this project you are working with shades of paints that are lighter or darker than the background and you may want to alter the balance. Apply the stencils when you are happy with the effect.

While daisies threaten the image of a perfect green lawn, daisy chains are, however, an important part of childhood, forming the basis for imaginative bracelets, necklaces and crowns. Later on, plucked single petals provide answers to whether 'he loves me or he loves me not'. Wild hedge roses do not lend themselves so readily to games. Their thorny wildness has a charm of its own. This stencil design combines the rigid qualities of the daisy and the rambling habit of the wild rose.

PROJECT PATTERN

Once you have stencilled the outside squares the centre is simply a daisy or rose bud. To achieve the rose, start with the bud stencil E and work the sepals stencil B on top.

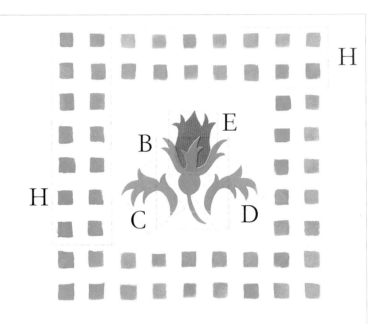

POSITIONING THE GINGHAM PATTERN

Plot the position of the pattern of squares by marking up a grid faintly in pencil. You can rub these lines out when you have finished stencilling, but make sure the paint is totally dry before you do so.

PROTECTING THE EDGES

Mask the edges of the headboard panels to protect the glazed woodwork from the stencil colours. Patching up smudged paintwork is virtually impossible unless you have applied a couple of layers of acrylic varnish, when you can usually gently wash off the smudge with a wet cloth.

ADDING PINK TIPS TO THE PETALS

To emphasize the daisy petal edges and give them a bit more life, it is fun to add a deep pink to the tips. Do this once the white paint is totally dry, so that the ends are blushed with colour.

DAISY & WILD ROSE BUDS VARIATIONS

These rose buds lend themselves to a retro 1950s wallpaper style. Put the stencils on a duck-egg blue, mint green or pale yellow background and use pinks and reds for the rose buds themselves. Link daisies into chains to create a linear pattern that could adorn any number of items. Stencils F and H can be combined into gingham stripes by slipping one over the other.

ALL-OVER DAISY CHAIN DESIGN (STENCILS A AND G)

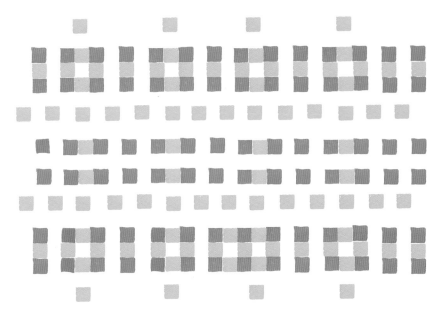

DOUBLE STRIPE (STENCIL H) WITH SINGLE STRIPE (STENCIL F)

DAISY CORNER (STENCIL A)

LEAF BORDER CORNER (STENCILS C AND D)

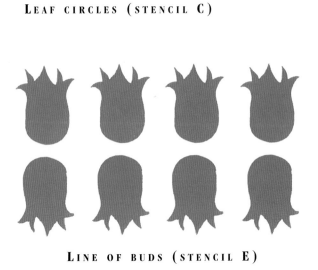

LEAF CIRCLES (STENCIL C)

LINE OF BUDS (STENCIL E)

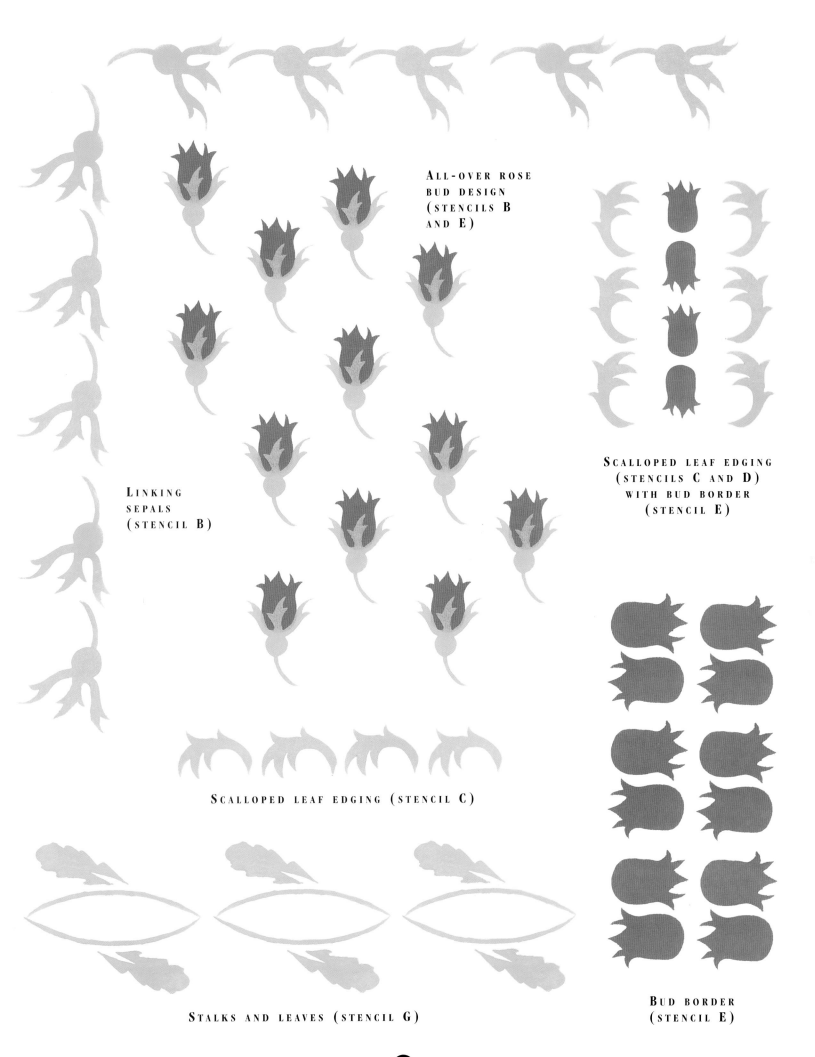

ALL-OVER ROSE
BUD DESIGN
(STENCILS B
AND E)

SCALLOPED LEAF EDGING
(STENCILS C AND D)
WITH BUD BORDER
(STENCIL E)

LINKING
SEPALS
(STENCIL B)

SCALLOPED LEAF EDGING (STENCIL C)

STALKS AND LEAVES (STENCIL G)

BUD BORDER
(STENCIL E)

23

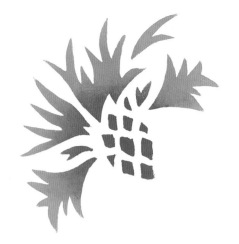

PAINT COLOUR GUIDE

Light blue   Deep blue

Forest green   Pine green

PAINTING THE FLOORBOARDS

1 Bare wood floors need to be well sanded before you can start painting. Start with a coarse sandpaper and gradually move on to finer grades once the really rough patches have been dealt with.

2 Apply a woodwash. Either buy a ready-made one or simply dilute white emulsion with water; it is a matter of trial and error to mix the density you require.

3 The wash dries extremely fast, so work with a single plank at a time to avoid join marks.

4 Follow the project pattern to apply the stencil design. Protect the floor afterwards with an oil-based wood varnish.

CORNFLOWERS & BUTTERFLIES

Cornflowers, bright blue thistle-like flowers with jagged petals, spindly stalks and long leaves, are visited by gentle butterflies in the design for this floor project. By painting the different elements in clean blues and greens on white woodwashed boards the feeling is of Scandinavian style. The large repeat allows the pattern to have an organic look, with leaves twisting and turning and the flowers stretching up to the sun. Butterflies hover and occasionally land to rest on a leaf.

PROJECT PATTERN

The pattern is built up using stencils A, C, D, E and F. Part of stencil E is repeated to provide a curly leaf to balance the design. The flanking leaf border is a simple repeat of stencil F.

TRACING THE PATTERN REPEAT
Having planned your pattern repeat, it can be useful to do a tracing of the entire repeat. Lift it up and down to check that all the elements of the design are in position and fit in the space you are tackling!

ADDING FORM TO THE LEAVES
To make your design look three-dimensional rather than flat, paint the leaves more realistically. Add a darker shade to the twists and underneath sections to give them a more rounded quality.

ADDING DETAIL WITH A BRUSH
Adding further detail by hand can give great lift to a design. In this project only the butterflies received this treatment. This technique can be useful to create a more hand-painted and individual look rather than simply using a repeated pattern.

CORNFLOWERS & BUTTERFLIES VARIATIONS

By simply curving the existing pattern repeat used in the floor project and adding a few leaves and butterflies you could create swags of spring flowers. Or just use single elements for a much simpler design, perhaps repeating a motif to establish an uncomplicated border. These stencil designs are very adaptable. A deep purple for the cornflower blooms goes well with sage green leaves and stems.

CORNFLOWER ROW (STENCILS A AND F)

LITTLE BUTTERFLIES (STENCIL D)

CURLING LEAVES STRIPE (STENCIL E)

CORNFLOWER FRIEZE (STENCIL A)

CURLING LEAVES BORDER (STENCIL E)

SWAG (STENCILS A, C, D, E AND F)

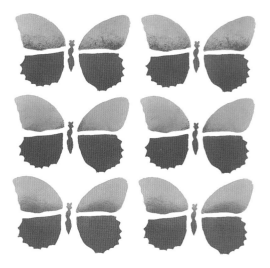

LINKING BUDS (STENCIL C)

BUTTERFLY STRIPES (STENCIL B)

LEAF LATTICE TILE (STENCIL F)

CURLING LEAVES BORDER (STENCIL E)
WITH LITTLE BUTTERFLIES (STENCIL D)

SIMPLE BUD REPEAT
(STENCIL C)

TWISTING LEAVES (STENCIL F)

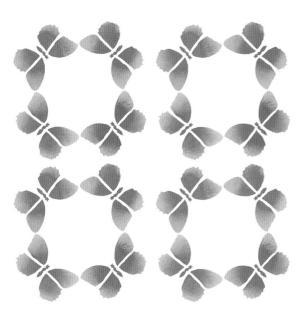

BUTTERFLY TILES (STENCIL B)

FRITILLARY

PAINT COLOUR GUIDE

Olive green	Dark forest green	Burgundy
White	Light terracotta	

PAINTING THE WALLS AND CURTAIN

1 First paint the walls in a yellow emulsion. Then add a wash of rich terracotta. The paint dries quickly and can look patchy if you are not careful, so work quite fast. It is easier working with two people.

2 Plan the entire design on paper and stick it to the wall to see the effect. This also helps you tackle the corners and work out joins, and where the flowers will stop before stencilling them.

3 The cream voile curtain is stencilled with white fabric paint. Put thick paper underneath the fabric and place paint pots on top to keep the stencil in place. Do not move the voile till the paint is dry.

Growing these majestic plants from seed can take seven years. Finding them in the wild is a real treat. When I was young I found a clump growing in a place only reachable by crawling under the prickly bushes at the end of my grandmother's garden. I thought I was the only person to have discovered them and guarded the secret closely. Years later I discovered that my grandmother had always admired their checkerboard petals and had especially kept that corner of the garden wild.

PROJECT PATTERN

To make the repeat build up two plants with leaves and flowers. Cut a reverse stencil of A to balance the composition of the stencil group.

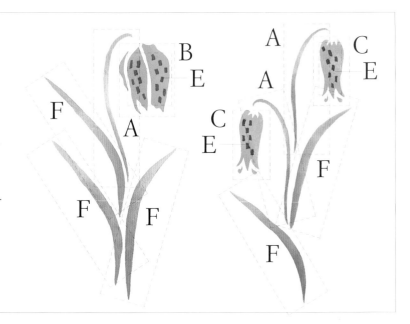

GRADATING COLOUR BY STIPPLING

By simply gradating a single colour you can create movement very easily. Here white is stippled on gently at first and then stronger colour is put on one side to give a more rounded quality.

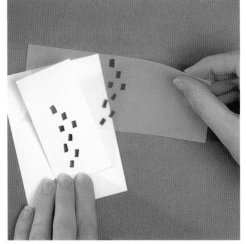

ACHIEVING THE CHECKERBOARD

It can be difficult to get the checkerboard effect in the right position. Trace the squares stencil E and their relation to the petals stencil B and use this drawing as a guide. Put the tracing in place and match the stencil to it, then remove the tracing.

ADDING TRANSLUCENCY

If you are using water-based paint and you want a more transparent look from your colours, try adding a little acrylic glaze to the paint. The glaze will help you spread the paint, leaving a more see-through effect.

FRITILLARY VARIATIONS

Frescos were traditionally painted straight onto freshly applied terracotta plasterwork. You can stick to solid colours or fade the colours at the edges so that the pattern is only a faint image with an aged or weathered appearance. Create a timeless quality by even missing out some parts. This pattern also lends itself to geometric interpretation, working from the checkerboard patterning on the bloom to achieve a symmetry.

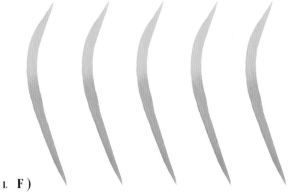

LEAF REPEAT (STENCIL F)

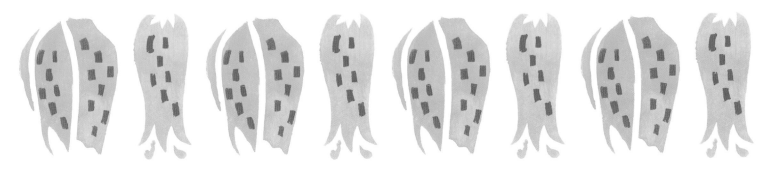

FLOWER HEADS (STENCILS B AND E, C AND E)

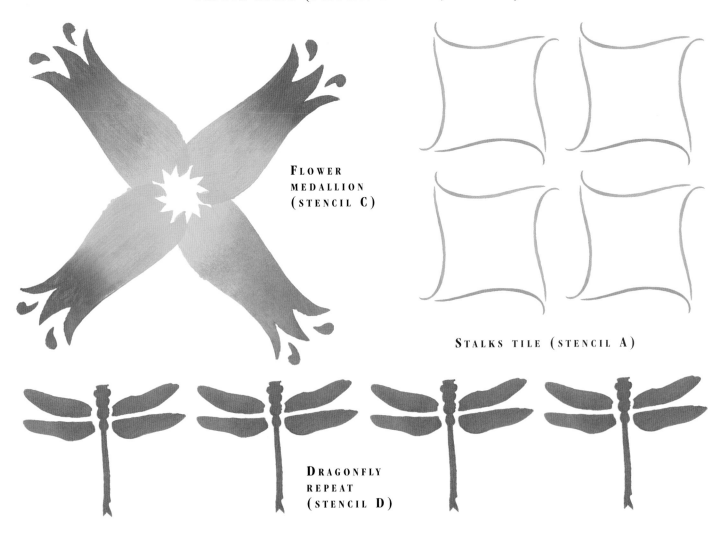

FLOWER MEDALLION (STENCIL C)

STALKS TILE (STENCIL A)

DRAGONFLY REPEAT (STENCIL D)

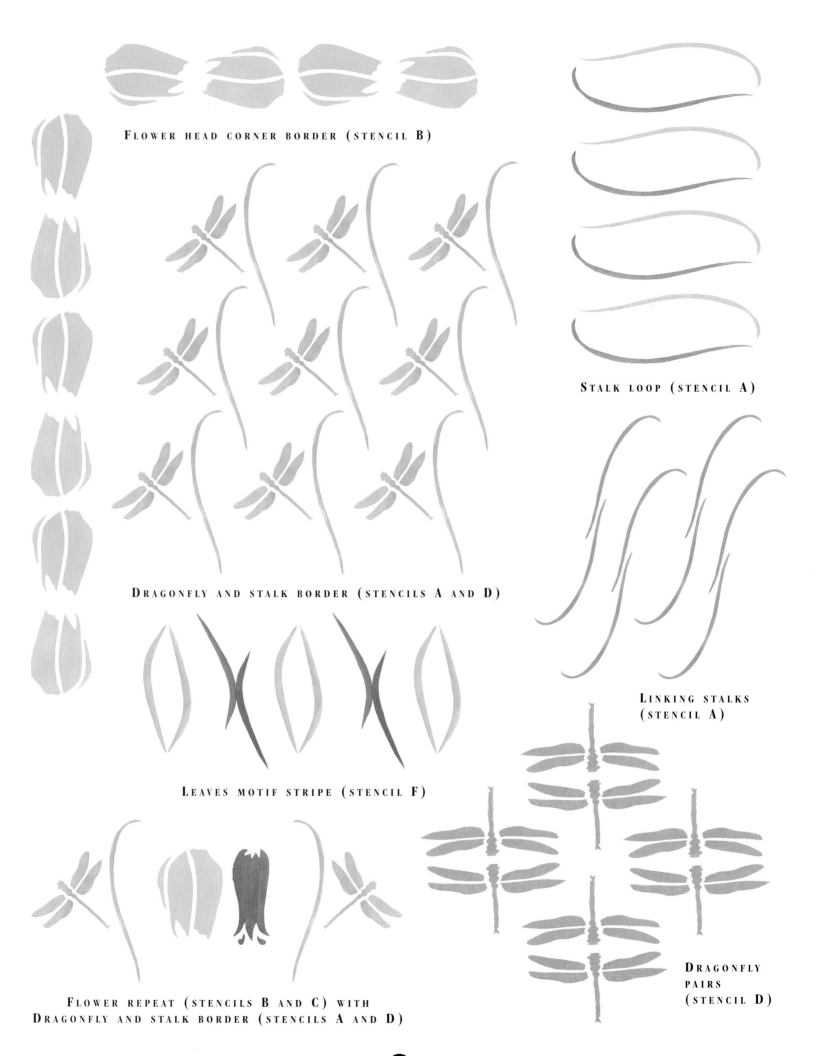

FLOWER HEAD CORNER BORDER (STENCIL B)

STALK LOOP (STENCIL A)

DRAGONFLY AND STALK BORDER (STENCILS A AND D)

LINKING STALKS (STENCIL A)

LEAVES MOTIF STRIPE (STENCIL F)

DRAGONFLY PAIRS (STENCIL D)

FLOWER REPEAT (STENCILS B AND C) WITH
DRAGONFLY AND STALK BORDER (STENCILS A AND D)

SUPPLIERS

Emulsion paints are easily obtainable from DIY stores and good hardware stores; contact manufacturers below for your nearest supplier. Oil sticks and acrylic paints can be obtained from artists' materials stores. Other stencilling supplies can usually be found in any of the above and there are many dedicated stencil stores.

Imperial Chemical Industries plc
(ICI)
(Dulux paints)
Wexham Road
Slough
SL2 5DS
(Tel. 01753 550000)

Crown Decorative Products
PO Box 37
Crown House
Hollins Road
Darwen
Lancashire
(Tel. 01254 704951)

Fired Earth plc
Twyford Mill
Oxford Road
Adderbury
Oxfordshire
(Tel. 01295 812088)

ACKNOWLEDGEMENTS

Thanks to Christophe Bourillon, Johnny and Siana Yewdall, Ben Stephens, Mum and Dad, Roy and Ellen, Kinnes and Baz, Anna and the Feel Good Studios.

First published in 1999 by Merehurst Limited
Ferry House, 51-57 Lacy Road, Putney, London SW15 1PR

© Copyright 1999 Merehurst Limited

ISBN 1-85391-732-X

A catalogue record of this book is available from the British Library.

Commissioning Editor: Anna Sanderson
Editor: Geraldine Christy
Designer: Roger Hammond
Photographer: Graeme Ainscough
Stylist: Caroline Davis

CEO & Publisher: Anne Wilson
International Sales Director: Mark Newman

Colour separation by Bright Arts (HK) Limited
Printed in Singapore

Katrina Hall divides her time between stencilling, paint effects and interior design for both commercial projects and private clients.

DANDELIONS

POPPIES

A

B

C

D

E

G

F —

Stencil F
is the inner
part of
stencil E

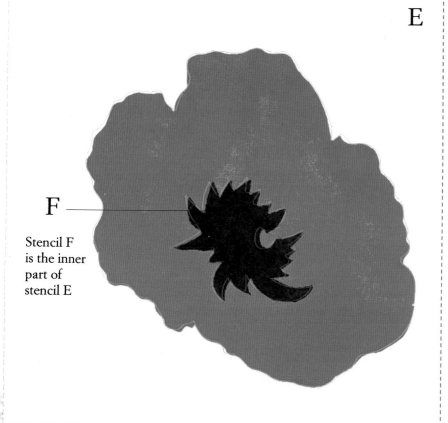

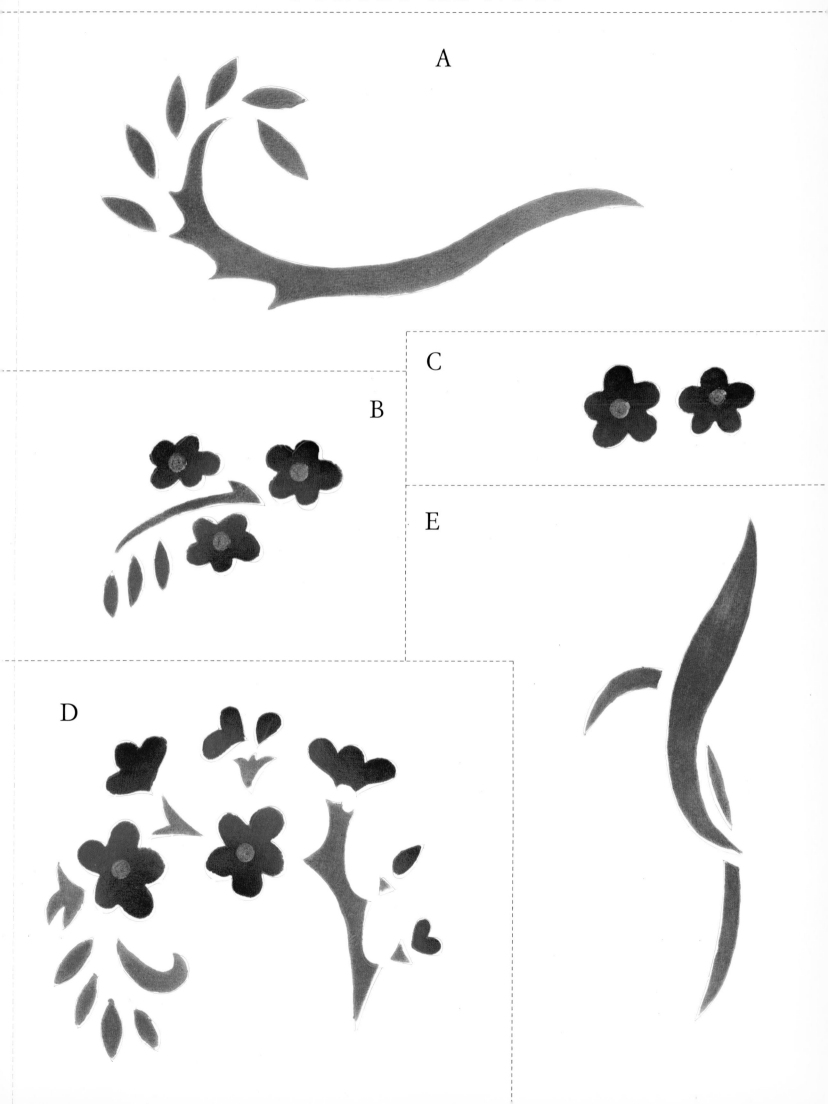

A

B

C

E

D

DAISY & WILD ROSE BUDS

 A

B

C

D

E

F

G

H

A

B

D

C

F

E

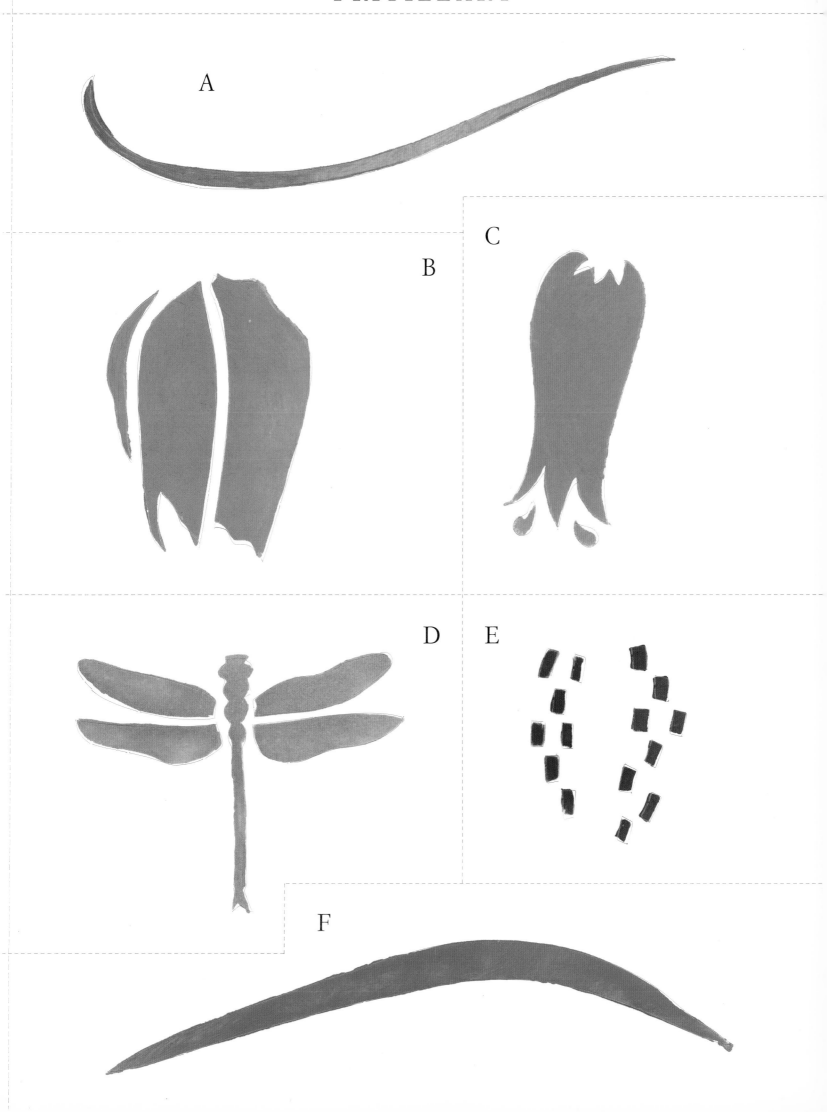

A

B

C

D

E

F